Want to know
history

Princesses

Suzan Boshouwers & Marjolein Hund

Clavis

NEW YORK

Look, Rose is in bed. She is very tired.
Today she played princess all day.
Rose knows everything about princesses.
She has a princess dress, a little crown, pumps,
and a palace with high towers. Rose falls asleep
and dreams that she is a real princess.

This is me

Hello, I am princess Rosemary. And this is my handmaiden. She helps me wash and dress every morning. First I take a bath. Then I put on my dress. It's quite a job!

I've got dresses to wear while eating, while dancing, and even while sleeping. Perhaps you wonder if I also have dresses to wear while playing. Well, usually I don't have much time to play.

I live in a big house with high towers. It's called a palace. I do not live in the same palace all the time. Sometimes I live in a holiday palace, sometimes in a party palace and sometimes in a winter palace.

This palace has almost hundred rooms. There are many people living and working here: cooks, servants, gardeners, stablemen, coachmen, guards, ladies-in-waiting, and many other people. I don't do much myself. However...

This is how I sit at the table

My father is the king and my mother is the queen.
Together they rule over the country.
That means that they make sure that all goes well.
Their work is very important
and they are often very busy.

Although there are times when I don't see
my parents for the whole day, we usually eat
together in the evenings. We sit at a big
table in the dining-hall. Sometimes –
like if there are important guests
visiting my parents – I eat with my
handmaiden in the children's room.

I have to behave nicely at the
table. Having good manners
is very important. "One can
recognize a real princess
by her good manners,"
my mother always says.

Did you know
I often have to sit still
for a long time? I let other
people speak before I can say
anything, and I have to behave
myself – just like you do.

This is how I learn new things

Princesses do not attend ordinary school. I have classes in the palace
and have a private tutor. That's not as much fun as it would be if I were in a class
with other children. Luckily my tutor teaches me a lot about our country and the world.

My tutor also teaches me to read, to write and to do math. I have other tutors too:
one who teaches me to embroider, one who teaches me to read notes and play
instruments, one who teaches me to dance, and one who teaches me to ride horseback.
All these are things a princess is supposed to do well.
As you can see, I've got a lot to learn!

Did you know
princes are supposed
to learn unusual things?
Things like archery
and fencing.

This is what my day looks like

I get up at half past seven. Before I put on my dress, I have to put on an undershirt, a petticoat, a shirt and a corset. My handmaiden helps me to dress. Sometimes I change clothes three times a day.

Right after breakfast I have princess class. I practice bowing, looking royal, walking down stairs in wide dresses, waving, and welcoming guests.

At eleven o'clock I have to pose for an artist. That means that I have to sit quietly while he paints my portrait. I have to be very still so the painter can see exactly what I look like.

At noon I have a history class. A princess has to know everything about the kings and queens of the past.

At half past three it is time for a piece of cake and a cup of tea. Look, I keep my little finger up when I hold my cup.

At half past four I go for a ride. I take lessons in riding with both my legs on the same side of the horse. It's called riding sidesaddle.

Before supper there is a little time left to play with my dog. He is my best friend. I tell him all my secrets.

At eight o'clock it is bedtime. That's the time when I can be alone with my mom and dad, and I like that.

This is how we celebrate

Today it is party time. It's my father's birthday! Flags are flying all over the country and there is a big parade! We ride through the streets in a coach.

Musicians walk up front, soldiers march behind them. Then comes our coach with the coachman. Can you see Granddad and Grandma? We are waving to the people along the road. They bow when we pass. When the parade is over, people celebrate on the streets. We have a big party at the palace.

This is how we have a ball

Now the ball begins! The whole palace is beautifully decorated and lit. Many kings and queens, princes and princesses have been invited. Some have traveled for days to get here. There is a big feast followed by dancing. The chandeliers are magnificent! The footmen have lit all the candles. There are two thousand of them!

Look what a gorgeous ball gown I am wearing! It was made especially for the ball and is decorated with glittering pearls and silver thread. Under the dress is a crinoline to keep the shape of the skirt. When the music starts, a prince asks me to dance. We dance together all night.

Did you know a princess only gets a real crown when she gets married?

This is how I say goodbye

That was the story of my life as a princess. I hope you enjoyed having a look inside the palace. Now I have to go to bed as it is already very late. I say goodbye to all the people at the feast. I give a big kiss to my mom and dad. "Goodnight, little princess," they say.

When I lie in my bed, I hear a little song far away. That is the song of the minstrel or the singer. It is old, but we still sing it, because it is so beautiful.

I had a lit-tle nut tree, no-thing would it bear   But a silver nutmeg   and a golden pear; The

King of Spain's daughter came to visit me, And all   for the sake of my little nut tree

I had a little nut tree

The King of Spain's daughter,
Came to visit me,
And all for the sake
Of my little nut tree.

Her dress was made of crimson,
Jet black was her hair,
She asked me for my nutmeg
And my golden pear

I said, "So fair a princess
Never did I see,
I'll give you all the fruit
From my little nut tree."

See you!

Which princess do you take after?

Princess Rosemary told you what the life of a princess was like in the past. But every princess is different. Have a look at these princesses. Just like you they all have their personalities. Which princess do you take after?

Princess Caraboo

Princess Caraboo was found on a square wearing beautiful silk clothes. When people asked who she was, she told them her name was Caraboo and that she was an eastern princess who had escaped from kidnappers. Later it turned out that she wasn't a princess at all, she was a maid!

If you take after princess Caraboo, you like to trick people. You are a brilliant actress and like to pretend.

Princess Anastasia

Princess Anastasia had eight different names. Sometimes she put on regular clothes and pretended to be an ordinary girl. When princess Anastasia got married, she wore such a big hat that no one could see her face. The prince couldn't even kiss her!

If you take after princess Anastasia, then you like hiding. Sometimes you like to pretend you're not there.

Princess Sisi

Princess Sisi only did what she wanted to do. She loved writing poems. She made sure that her face was never touched by the sun. She believed the paler her face, the more beautiful she was. On one of her birthdays her father gave her a special cake. When it was cut, real birds flew out!

If you take after princess Sisi, you don't like to be told what to do. And you love surprises!

Princess Cleopatra

Princess Cleopatra lived a very long time ago. She was famous for her beauty. Cleopatra lived in a magnificent palace by the sea and kept a snake as a pet. She refused to walk on the ground so servants had to carry her everywhere.

If you take after princess Cleopatra, you like to be well taken care of. Remember though, it's important to be nice to other people!

Princess Kalina

Kalina means "wild rose". She was born a princess, but became queen at the age of six. Her father decided to send her to a regular school. She was wild about bees and knew everything about honey. At her wedding, thousands of rose petals fluttered from the ceiling of the palace.

If you take after princess Kalina, you love nature and animals.

Princess Pocahontas

Princess Pocahontas has been called an "American Princess". She was the daughter of a Native American chief and she married an English settler. She did a lot to make peace between her people and the settlers.

If you take after Pocahontas, you don't like quarrels. If people don't get on, you try to make peace.

Cupcakes fit for a princess

Tip
Make a cup of tea and drink it with your pinkie out!

This is what you need:
12 cupcakes (make them from your favorite recipe or buy them readymade)

2 tubs white frosting
Food coloring
A variety of toppings like: coconut flakes, chopped nuts, colored sprinkles, colored sugar, chopped chocolate, etc.

This is what you should do:
Divide the white frosting into several small bowls. Add a few drops of food coloring to each bowl. Mix well. Add a different color to each bowl until you have a selection of different colors.

Put the toppings into several small bowls or plates.

Make sure the cupcakes are cool before you start frosting. Use a small butter knife or spatula to cover the tops of the cupcakes with frosting of your choice. You can combine colors if you like! Now comes the really fun part. Hold the cupcakes by the bottoms and dip the frosted tops into the bowls of coconut, sprinkles, nuts, chocolate or whatever you choose.

Put your cupcakes on a tiered cake server or special serving plate.

Make your own bracelet

This is what you need:
The most beautiful buttons and beads you can find
Two colors of ribbon
Velcro

Tip
A princess is not a real princess without jewels, so think about making a matching necklace! You can use small pearls instead of buttons.

This is what you do:
Twist the ribbons around each other. Tie a knot every so often. Thread on a button after every knot and then tie another knot. Attach Velcro to each end so the bracelet will close.

What delicious food!

Mini-quiz

1. Do you think a princess gets many letters?

2. Does a princess have to dress herself?

3. What does a princess learn from her tutor?

4. What does a princess practice during her princess classes?

5. Do you think that a princess gets bored now and then?

6. Do princesses play hide and seek?

7. Are princesses good dancers?

8. When does a princess get her first real crown?

9. Do princesses like to pose for painters?

10. Name a few animals that live in the palace.

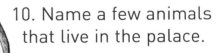